SUPER SIMPLE
EARTH INVESTIGATIONS

SUPER SIMPLE
EARTHQUAKE
PROJECTS

Science Activities for
Future Seismologists

JESSIE ALKIRE

CONSULTING EDITOR, DIANE CRAIG, M.A./READING SPECIALIST

Super Sandcastle

An Imprint of Abdo Publishing
abdopublishing.com

abdopublishing.com

Published by Abdo Publishing, a division of ABDO, PO Box 398166, Minneapolis, Minnesota 55439. Copyright © 2018 by Abdo Consulting Group, Inc. International copyrights reserved in all countries. No part of this book may be reproduced in any form without written permission from the publisher. Super SandCastle™ is a trademark and logo of Abdo Publishing.

Printed in the United States of America, North Mankato, Minnesota
102017
012018

THIS BOOK CONTAINS RECYCLED MATERIALS

Design: Kelly Doudna, Mighty Media, Inc.
Production: Mighty Media, Inc.
Editor: Liz Salzmann
Cover Photographs: Mighty Media, Inc.; Shutterstock
Interior Photographs: Courtesy of the Archives, California Institute of Technology; Mighty Media, Inc.; Shutterstock

The following manufacturers/names appearing in this book are trademarks: Artist's Loft™, Nice!™, Pillsbury Creamy Supreme®, Pyrex®, Sharpie®

Publisher's Cataloging-in-Publication Data

Names: Alkire, Jessie, author.
Title: Super simple earthquake projects: science activities for future seismologists / by Jessie Alkire.
Other titles: Science activities for future seismologists
Description: Minneapolis, Minnesota : Abdo Publishing, 2018. | Series: Super simple earth investigations
Identifiers: LCCN 2017946431 | ISBN 9781532112362 (lib.bdg.) | ISBN 9781614799788 (ebook)
Subjects: LCSH: Seismology--Juvenile literature. | Earthquakes--Juvenile literature. | Science--Experiments--Juvenile literature.
Classification: DDC 507.8--dc23
LC record available at https://lccn.loc.gov/2017946431

Super SandCastle™ books are created by a team of professional educators, reading specialists, and content developers around five essential components–phonemic awareness, phonics, vocabulary, text comprehension, and fluency–to assist young readers as they develop reading skills and strategies and increase their general knowledge. All books are written, reviewed, and leveled for guided reading and early reading intervention programs for use in shared, guided, and independent reading and writing activities to support a balanced approach to literacy instruction.

TO ADULT HELPERS

The projects in this title are fun and simple. There are just a few things to remember to keep kids safe. Some projects require the use of sharp or hot objects. Also, kids may be using messy materials such as glue or paint. Make sure they protect their clothes and work surfaces. Review the projects before starting, and be ready to assist when necessary.

KEY SYMBOLS

Watch for these warning symbols in this book. Here is what they mean.

HOT!
You will be working with something hot. Get help!

SHARP!
You will be working with a sharp object. Get help!

CONTENTS

WHAT IS AN EARTHQUAKE?

An earthquake is when the ground shakes. It begins deep beneath Earth's surface. An earthquake can cause a lot of **damage**.

EARTHQUAKE DAMAGE

There is sometimes a **sequence** of three earthquake stages.

FORESHOCKS

The first stage is foreshocks. These are small quakes that occur before a larger one. But a quake isn't called a foreshock until a larger one happens after it.

MAIN SHOCK

The second stage is the main shock. It is larger than any of its foreshocks. The main shock can be very **dangerous**. It can cause large structures to fall down.

AFTERSHOCKS

The third stage is aftershocks. These are smaller quakes that follow the main shock. Aftershocks can happen weeks or months after the main shock. Some continue for years!

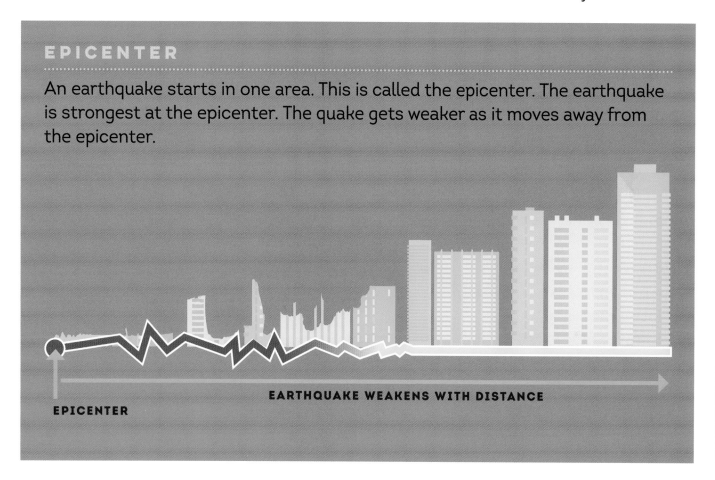

EPICENTER

An earthquake starts in one area. This is called the epicenter. The earthquake is strongest at the epicenter. The quake gets weaker as it moves away from the epicenter.

EPICENTER

EARTHQUAKE WEAKENS WITH DISTANCE

WHAT CAUSES EARTHQUAKES?

Earth's crust is made up of pieces called tectonic plates. Tectonic plates move slowly. This movement causes earthquakes. The plates move three different ways. This creates three types of boundaries between the plates.

CONVERGENT BOUNDARY

Some plates move toward each other. They press together. One plate may slide under the other plate. This can cause mountains to form. The Cascade Range in western North America was formed this way.

DIVERGENT BOUNDARY

Some plates move away from each other. The space between the plates is called a rift. **Magma** may rise from under Earth's crust to fill the space. Some rifts get filled with ocean water.

TRANSFORM BOUNDARY

Some plates move sideways. They grind against each other. The San Andreas Fault in California is an example of this type of movement. Earthquakes are common there.

HOW SCIENTISTS STUDY EARTHQUAKES

Some scientists study earthquakes. They are called seismologists.

Scientists use a tool called a seismograph. Seismographs measure any movement of Earth's surface. The movement is recorded as lines on paper. During an earthquake, the lines get longer.

The size of the lines tells seismologists how large a quake is. The size of an earthquake is called its **magnitude**.

SEISMOGRAPH

CHARLES FRANCIS RICHTER

Charles Francis Richter was a seismologist. He spent most of his life in California. The state has many earthquakes. Richter studied earthquakes during and after college. He created a new earthquake scale in 1935. It is called the Richter Scale. The scale measures earthquake **magnitude**.

US QUAKE ZONES

In the United States, most earthquakes occur in Alaska and California. But there are other areas that are also likely to have earthquakes. Seismologists help people learn how to prepare for and survive earthquakes.

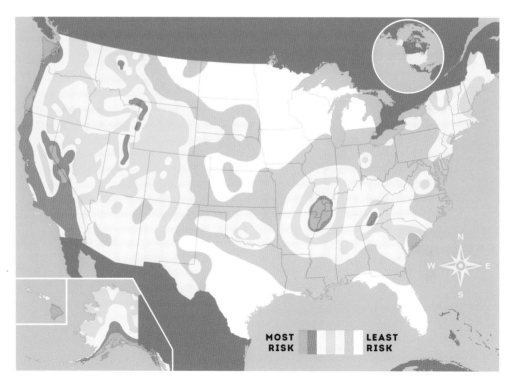

MOST RISK   LEAST RISK

MATERIALS

Here are some of the materials that you will need for the projects in this book.

ALUMINUM FOIL   **BRICK**   **CARDBOARD BOX**   **FOOD COLORING**   **FUNNEL**   **GELATIN**

GRAHAM CRACKERS   **HAMMER**   **MASKING TAPE**   **MEASURING CUP**   **MINI MARSHMALLOWS**   **NAILS**

PAINT PENS

PAPER CLIPS

PAPER FASTENERS

PEBBLES

PITCHER

PLASTIC BOTTLE

PLASTIC CONTAINER

RUBBER SPATULA

SOUP OR VEGETABLE CAN

SQUARE GLASS BAKING DISH

TOOTHPICKS

VANILLA FROSTING

TIPS AND TECHNIQUES

There are many ways to create the effect of an earthquake. You just need an unstable surface. Gelatin works well. So does soil or sand. You could also use a mattress. Set objects on the unstable surface and then shake or hit the surface. Do the objects fall over?

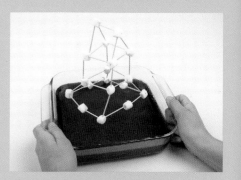

GRAHAM CRACKER TECTONIC PLATES

MATERIALS: vanilla frosting, bowl, red food coloring, rubber spatula, 3 plastic plates, 6 graham cracker squares

Y ou learned about tectonic plates and how they move on pages 6 and 7. Now explore the differences between these movements using graham crackers and frosting!

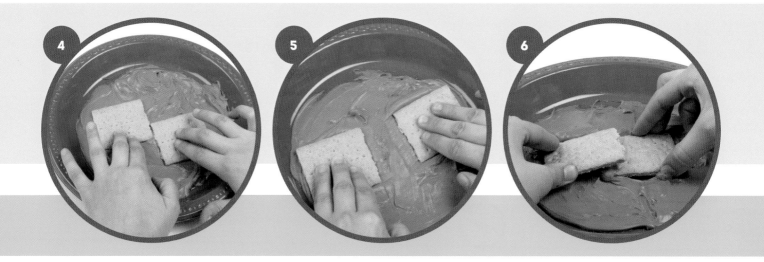

① Put the frosting in a bowl. Add several drops of red food coloring. Mix well.

② Spread a layer of frosting on each plastic plate. This is **magma**.

③ Place two graham crackers next to each other on each plate. The crackers are tectonic plates.

④ On the first plate, move the crackers in opposite directions sideways. Make them grind against each other. This is a transform boundary.

⑤ On the second plate, press down gently on the graham crackers and move them apart. This is a divergent boundary.

⑥ On the third plate, push one graham cracker under the other cracker. This is a convergent boundary. The area where the plates cross is called a subduction zone.

⑦ Enjoy a frosting and graham crackers snack!

SEISMIC WAVE BOX

MATERIALS: cardboard box, craft knife (optional), nail, ruler, string, scissors, clear tape, paper clips

Seismic waves are waves of energy. They are created when tectonic plates slip past one another. The waves cause shaking during earthquakes.

① If the box has flaps, have an adult help you cut them off with a craft knife.

② Set the box on its side. Use a nail to poke holes in the top and bottom of the box. Make sure the holes are directly across from each other.

③ Measure the height of the box. Cut a piece of string a few inches longer than the measurement.

④ Thread the string through the holes in the box. Tape the ends of the string to the outside of the box. Make sure the string is **taut**.

⑤ Secure paper clips to the string. Space them evenly apart.

⑥ Set the box on a table. Hit or push the table. This produces energy waves. The waves travel from the table to the box to the string. This should cause the paper clips to quiver. If they don't, try to push or hit the table harder.

SEISMOGRAPH

MATERIALS: soup or vegetable can, hammer, nail, pen, cardboard, scissors, paper fastener, masking tape, marker that is as tall as the can, ruler, aluminum foil, paper

Seismologists measure an earthquake's **magnitude** with a seismograph. The seismograph draws lines representing seismic waves. When the waves get bigger or smaller, so do the seismograph lines.

1 Use a hammer and nail to make a hole in the center of the bottom of the can.

2 Trace the bottom of the can on a piece of cardboard. Cut the circle out.

③ Use the nail to poke a hole in the center of the cardboard circle.

④ Place the circle on the bottom of the can.

5 Push a paper fastener through the holes in the cardboard and the can.

⑥ Bend the ends of the paper fastener inside the can. Don't press them tightly against the can. The cardboard circle should spin freely.

Continued on the next page.

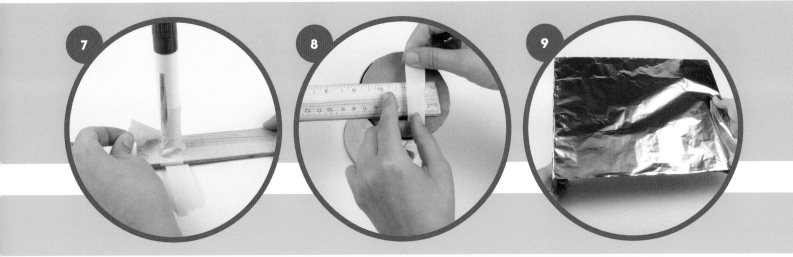

7 Stand a marker upright on the end of a ruler. The cap should point up. Tape it in place.

8 Turn the ruler over so the marker points down. Tape the opposite end of the ruler to the cardboard circle.

9 Cover a large piece of cardboard with aluminum foil. Secure the foil with tape.

10 Place a piece of paper on the foil.

11 Take the cap off the marker.

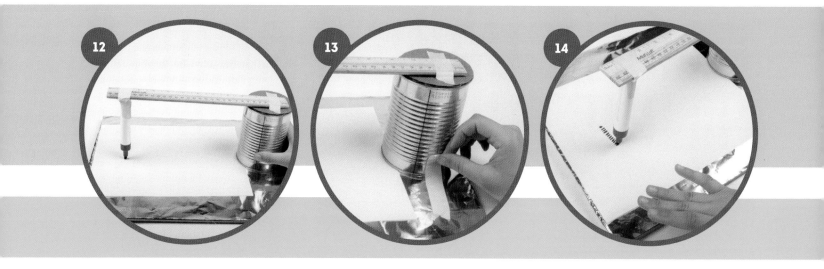

12 Place the can so the tip of the marker touches the paper.

13 Tape the can to the foil.

14 Tap on the foil-covered cardboard. Watch the lines the marker makes.

15 Try tapping harder or softer. How do the lines compare?

EARTHQUAKE-PROOF STRUCTURES

MATERIALS: 6-ounce (170 g) gelatin package, large bowl, measuring cup, water, mixing spoon, square glass baking dish, toothpicks, mini marshmallows, notebook, pen

Strong earthquakes can cause a lot of **damage**. They can destroy homes, buildings, roads, and more.

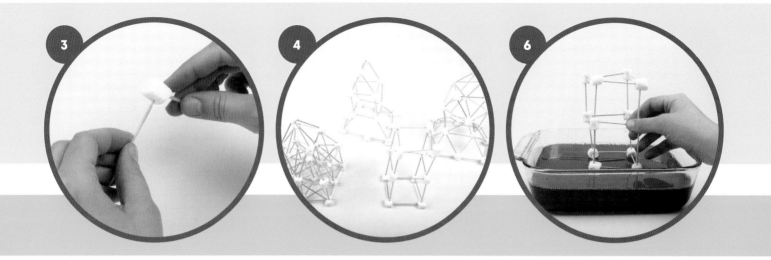

① Ask an adult to help you mix the gelatin. Follow the directions on the package.

② Pour the gelatin into the glass baking dish. Refrigerate for four hours or until set.

③ While the gelatin is setting, connect toothpicks together with mini marshmallows.

④ Build several toothpick and marshmallow structures. Make them different sizes and shapes.

⑤ When the gelatin has set, remove it from the refrigerator.

⑥ Place one of your structures on the gelatin.

Continued on the next page.

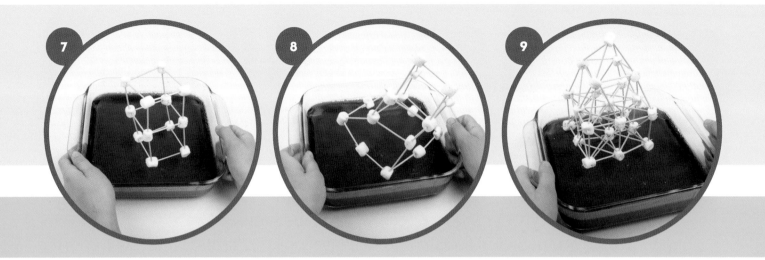

7 Shake the dish for ten seconds. What happens to the structure?

8 Put a different structure on the gelatin and shake it. Did the same thing happen?

9 Test the remaining structures the same way.

10 Write what happened to each structure in a notebook.

11 Think about why the structures moved differently on the shaking gelatin. Was it because of the shape or size? What could you do to make them more stable?

DIGGING DEEPER

Earthquakes often move buildings from side to side. Builders include features to resist this motion. The goal of most of these features is to let the building sway slightly. This makes it harder for a quake to knock it down.

COMPUTER-CONTROLLED WEIGHTS ON THE ROOF

The computer detects which way the quake moves the building. Then it tells the weights to move in the opposite direction. This helps the building resist the force of the quake.

FLEXIBLE STEEL FRAME

The frame holds the building together. But it can move enough for the building to sway a little.

SHOCK ABSORBERS

Rubber bases on the foundation **absorb** the force of the quake. This reduces its effect.

DEEP FOUNDATION

The building's **foundation** is in **bedrock**. This makes the building extra sturdy.

LIQUEFACTION EXPERIMENT

MATERIALS: plastic container, sand, pitcher, water, brick, paint pens

Earthquakes can affect structures that are on wet soil. The quake's movement causes the wet soil to act more like a liquid. This is called liquefaction. Liquefaction weakens buildings' **foundations**. This can cause buildings to fall down.

① Place the plastic container on a table. Fill the container three-fourths full of sand.

② Pour water to almost the top of the sand.

③ Use paint pens to make the brick look like a building. Draw on windows and a door.

④ Set the brick in the sand so it stands up.

⑤ Knock on the sides of the container. What happens to the sand? What about the building? This process is liquefaction!

⑥ Try knocking harder or softer. What happens?

TSUNAMI IN A BOTTLE

MATERIALS: large plastic bottle, funnel, pebbles, ruler, measuring cup, water, blue food coloring

Earthquakes can occur underwater. These quakes can move the seafloor and create powerful waves. These waves are called tsunamis. The waves can reach land and cause a lot of harm.

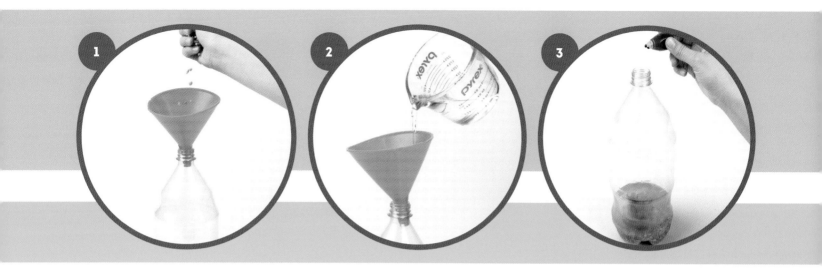

1 Use a funnel to fill the bottle with about 2 inches (5 cm) of pebbles.

2 Fill the bottle with about 4 inches (10 cm) of water.

3 Add one drop of blue food coloring.

Continued on the next page.

4 Secure the cap tightly.

5 Carefully lower the bottle to its side. The pebbles are the seafloor. The water is the ocean.

6 Hit the bottom of the bottle. This creates a wave like a tsunami.

7 Hit the bottle harder and softer. Observe how the waves change.

DIGGING DEEPER

A tsunami is a series of large ocean waves. They can be caused by an underwater earthquake. The movement of the plates on the ocean floor creates the tsunami waves. They aren't like normal ocean waves. Tsunami waves can move at hundreds of miles per hour. They can be more than 100 feet (30 m) tall! When the waves crash onto land, they knock down buildings and create floods. Tsunamis usually last for several hours. But some can last for days!

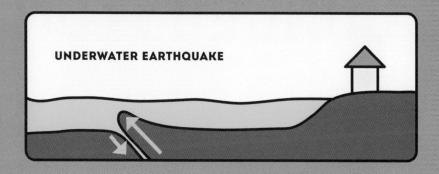

UNDERWATER EARTHQUAKE

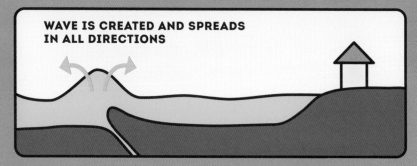

WAVE IS CREATED AND SPREADS IN ALL DIRECTIONS

WAVE CRASHES ONTO LAND

CONCLUSION

Earthquakes occur when tectonic plates move. This can cause harm to people and structures. Seismologists study earthquakes. They help people stay safe during quakes.

QUIZ

1. Most main shocks are followed by aftershocks.
   TRUE OR FALSE?

2. What are the pieces that make up Earth's crust called?

3. What is an earthquake's strength called?

LEARN MORE ABOUT IT!

You can find out more about earthquakes at the library. Or you can ask an adult to help you **research** earthquakes **online**!

Answers: 1. True 2. Tectonic plates 3. Magnitude

GLOSSARY

absorb – to keep a force from having an effect.

bedrock – the solid rock beneath soil and looser rock.

damage – harm or ruin.

dangerous – able or likely to cause harm or injury.

foundation – the base or support upon which a building rests.

magma – melted rock below Earth's surface.

magnitude – the size or importance of something, such as an earthquake.

online – connected to the Internet.

research – to find out more about something.

sequence – a group of things that come one after the other.

taut – pulled or stretched tight.